Snow in New York

Snow in New York

New and Selected Poems

Matthew Brennan

LITERARY PRESS
LAMAR UNIVERSITY

ISBN: 978-1-942956-87-7
Library of Congress Number: 2021936365

Cover image credit:
Snow in New York, after Henri,
by Suzanne Brennan

Lamar University Literary Press
Beaumont, Texas

Acknowledgments and Author's Note

Poems selected from *Seeing in the Dark* (Hawkhead Press, 1993) and from *The House with the Mansard Roof* (The Backwaters Press, 2009) are reprinted by permission of Matthew Brennan, the copyright holder. Many thanks to the publishers, David Vancil and Greg Kosmicki.

I am also thankful to the publishers of the following books (copyrighted under my name) for permission to reprint poems or excerpts: *The Music of Exile* (Cloverdale Books-Wyndham Hall Press, 1994); *The Sea-Crossing of Saint Brendan* (Birch Brook Press, 2008); and *One Life* (Lamar University Literary Press, 2016). Special thanks to Tom Tolnay, Jerry Craven, and Theresa Ener.

The selected poems were first published in *Blue Unicorn, California Quarterly, Cape Rock, Cloverdale Review of Criticism and Poetry, Commonweal, Concho River Review, descant, Elder Mountain, Green Hills Literary Lantern, Iambs & Trochees, Journal of Kentucky Studies, Kansas Quarterly, Kentucky Poetry Review, Light Quarterly, Louisville Review, Merton Seasonal, Mid-America Poetry Review, Mildred, Mississippi Valley Review, New Mexico Humanities Review, Notre Dame Review, Passages North, Paterson Literary Review, Phoebe, Pivot, Poem, Poet Lore, Poetry Ireland Review, San Pedro River Review, Sewanee Review, South Carolina Review, South Dakota Review, Southern Indiana Review, Sycamore Review, Tipton Poetry Journal, Trinacria, War, Literature and the Arts, Watching the Perseids: The Backwaters Press Twentieth Anniversary Anthology, Webster Review, Westview, Wind,* and *Yalobusha Review.* I remain grateful to the editors of these publications.

Thanks also to the editors of the following journals where the new poems were first published: *Blue Unicorn, Concho River Review, The Galway Review, Green Hills Literary Lantern, Heartland Review, Last Stanza Poetry Journal, Paterson Literary Review, Poem, Poetry Ireland Review, Tipton Poetry Journal,* and *Valparaiso Poetry Review.*

This collection comprises poems written since 1977. The three poems from that year are "Noon Glare," "Dover in December," and "Seeing in the Dark." The new poems were written from 2016 through 2020. "Winter Landscape," reprinted in *The Ekphrastic Review*, won a Fantastic Ekphrastic Award for contribution to ekphrastic literature.

I have arranged the selections here chronologically by book, but seven poems in the first two books reappear in subsequent collections, most of the time in revised form; while placing all poems in their original contexts, I have reprinted their most recent incarnations.

The Sea-Crossing of Saint Brendan is a verse re-telling, not a translation, of *Navigatio Sancti Brendani Abbatis*, a Latin prose narrative that appeared in Ireland in the ninth century. My version employs an approximation of the Anglo-Saxon alliterative meter found in the Germanic medieval epic *Beowulf*.

For the love of my life, Beverley;
my grandchildren, Ava and Cannon;
their parents, my son Dan and daughter-in-law Brittany;
and in memory of my parents,
Suzanne Simon Brennan and William J. Brennan

Other Works by Matthew Brennan

Poetry |

Seeing in the Dark
The Music of Exile
American Scenes (chapbook)
The Sea-Crossing of Saint Brendan
The House with the Mansard Roof
The Light of Common Day (chapbook)
One Life

Criticism |

Wordsworth, Turner, and Romantic Landscape
The Gothic Psyche
The Poet's Holy Craft
The Colosseum Critical Introduction to Dana Gioia

CONTENTS

From *Seeing in the Dark* |1993

Seeing in the Dark

Below my father's house, lies a river valley
where the Mississippi rolls, lifting mist
in the morning till sunlight consumes it,
slowly, the way dogs dally round dishes
when watched. At night, barge-warnings
echo up the bluff and die at our doorstep.
Sometimes, if the moon strikes you right,
and the cold air smells clean, the night pulls
you inward before you can stop
and, as you're swallowed, turns
you inside out—there
                              in darkness
blindness becomes sight, and you see
how the world looks to those dying,
before first dawn light, when the moon
is glowing like a darkroom lamp
and the landscape is a negative,
undeveloped, waiting for
immersion.

Noon Glare

By rays that are sharper than the sharpest angle
Of cut glass in a jeweler's shop, noon glare
Refracts the traffic lights and no dew drops
Moisten front lawns, no shade cools screened-in porches.
Now, beams strip the neighborhood bare and blister
Drab clapboards, day lilies, and asphalt drives.
You watch exhaust filter into the haze
That hangs there like sauna steam; you daydream.
You think of the dusk breeze in the park and recall
The lust, last fall, that colored her cheeks pink.
But autumn has its dullness, too, you know,
For even in its dying, bleeding prism,
The sun can splash on any windshield's glass,
Blinding as daybreak in Sahara glares.

Dover in December
(An American's Dream of a Married Christmas in Calais)

I
Last autumn was the wettest in English history
since 1727 when Fielding wrote his comedy,
Love in Several Masques, in which he tried "to laugh
mankind out of their favourite follies and vices."
After the lonely Thanksgiving in a Chinese restaurant,
the sky trembled, swelling solid, ripe and black
as gargantuan cherry clusters, ever ready
to rupture its bowels or, if constipated,
to belly out guffaws of thunderstorms and fire.

II
Then December fell and winter with it.
The first day, "the cold was invigorating."
The frost that iced the green grass and stripped trees
and the steel-blue sky streaked with frozen clouds
ground tranquility with blood and bone-marrow.
Through the brisk air glided white pigeons and ravens,
and, opposite the setting sun, a ghost-like moon,
conforming to her image, rose in the east.

III
Nightfall swallowed the landscape
and the sun-filtered mist, blackening eyes
with anxiety about frostbite and lost limbs,
while the wind swept over the sill,
fanning curtains and turning pink flesh blue.
Rustling fully clothed, plus Shetland sweater
and stocking cap, shrouded in Edinburgh blankets,
the shape shivered into sleep.

IV

It was just before Christmas, southeast of London.
He climbed to the roof of Dover Castle, where,
from a tower, he watched sunlight refracted by clouds
land on the Channel and blur the fusion of sky and sea.
The past was lost in the present till, like the Celtics,
he caught, beyond the edge of a dry white crag,
Scandinavian vessels veer in and out of harbor:
Next week, he mused, his prow, too, maneuvering whitecaps,
would come in her port in Calais, early Christmas morning.

A Divorcée's Revenge

Hearing your poisoned voice again today
Makes me think of the great Christian martyrs
Like Agatha who, when ripped from sackcloth
And sandals, raped, then raped again, and rolled
Over forty feet of burning coals,
Never once lost her smile—not until blisters
Blurred what had been her lips. And I as well
Won't budge: You hate my "Goddamned guts" for what
I've got and won't give up—our kids, my neck.
But now I've cut the wires, to keep my cool,
And love all the wide world that is not you.

A Woman Fishing

Another day is ending in northern Minnesota,
Where a widow, alone in a lifeboat, is
Drifting, far from shore, on the still waters of a deep lake.

Soon, the woman's dark form becomes a silhouette
Against the amber of the far distance
That gleams with the last light of the buried sun.

As if she'd waited all day for this one moment,
When the day is dead but the long night
Is not yet born, and the ghostly moon is not awake,

Now, for a few seconds only, she feels again
The glow of her husband, the single being
Whose life she's loved for fifty years, whose pole

She now holds like a blind woman's cane,
Casting into that cold, endless darkness.

Sky Lights

When my grandmother died, sky—
white as if embalmed—buried
roads and parking lots with snow.
The next day, though, as we drove
to her grave in north St. Louis,
the sun penetrated ice like light
pulsing through glass tubes.

I remembered then a hot June night,
months before. Late, I'd walked
by a huge house lit from rathskeller
to rafters, Mozart thundering
through its open door, while above
stars splintered like bones withdrawing
into the cold folds of earth.

Resurrection

My job these days is to cut lumber
at the Ace Hardware store. Often, too,
I do the inventory. It is then
when the past comes back and I need
to go home, build a small fire,
and watch the logs go up in smoke,
dead trees transformed into something else.
In Nam, my job was to bring back
the bodies on flatbed trucks, stacked
in rows like cords of wood. Sometimes,
if a mine blew up in a muddy
rice field where five men had crouched
in soupy water, blood would flood
them like a bouillabaisse—we'd fish
out what we could. But once,
when a ship got bombed off harbor
in water clear as a mirror, I went
down to count the dead, then sent them
upwards, one by one, like balloons
let go, allowed at last to rise
in the light like motes of yellow dust.

From *The Music of Exile* | 1994

The Music of Exile

A Rachmaninoff *Prelude* penetrates
The walls from the next apartment
And suddenly my mind opens
Like ground split by an earthquake,
So once again I see, if not quite feel,
What life then was really like
When, one Saturday in August, in 1959,
I barged into the kitchen
Where a piano played on the radio
And beneath the single fluorescent light
My parents—Dad sweating from yard work,
Mom aproned for cooking—abruptly
Embraced, and I stood there, embarrassed
But fiercely happy, not yet aware
That the winter night when Moscow fell
Rachmaninoff fled Russia, forever.

The Wolf

Late in the night, long after the moon set,
When air got bone-cold and deep dreams began,
We'd suddenly be wakened by great groans
Thundering through white plaster walls, bolting
From the snot clotted in my father's throat
That made his drunk snoring sound like wolf-howls
Heaved from a trap in the Wyoming rocks.

Once, in a dream, through my window I heard
Growls of a wolf at prey, and woke so choked
With fear, though I screamed with all my might,
No noise came out, just air.
                              Eight years later,
My father had cancer but no one knew.
He'd moan in his sleep, shaking the whole house
With each wild eruption of breath, till pain
Broke out in one long penetrating roar—
But I have never budged, not then, not now.
Late at night I always keep my distance:
The wolf is inside him.

August Morning in Bloom's Bay

All that summer you'd suffered.
Afternoons, you trudged, to kill time,
Around a brown field behind the house
Where anthills sprouted like athlete's foot
Among stunted clumps of ragweed and shrubs.
Earth, each time you lunged forward, cracked
Open wider, craving for water. At night,
When twilight, at last, had smoldered,
A sky of black syrup began to drip
Down, and the cracks closed up like morning glories.

But when darkness itself moved through the heat
And crickets were singing, *a cappella*,
As if human sadness clung to their notes,
Nothing foreshadowed
The luminous August morning you'd watch
From the Jersey shore, where a channel juts
Inland like a woman and enfolds the light
Till everything, as far as you can see,
Shines.

Nights Our House Comes to Life

Some nights in midwinter when the creek clogs
With ice and the spines of fir trees stiffen
Under a blank, frozen sky,
On these nights our house comes to life.
It happens when you're half asleep.
A sudden crack, a fractured dream, you bolting
Upright—but all you can hear is the clock
Your great-grandfather found in 1850
And smuggled here from Dublin for his future bride,
A being as unknown to him then as she is now
To you, a being as distant as the strangers
Who built this house, and died in this room
Some cold, still night, like tonight,
When all that was heard were the rhythmic clicks
Of a pendulum, and something, barely audible,
Moving in the dark on the attic stairs.

Winter Scene, Past Midnight

Past midnight, long after lovemaking,
The light patter of snow,
Like the voice of a dead child or parent,
Taps at the panes and abruptly wakes you.
You go to the window that opens
To the park of oaks and, beyond,
To the art museum's portico—
Through frost you see no moon, just clouds
Arched low like a blown-glass bowl.

You lift the window, lean into the cold,
And try to remember what you were dreaming
When, moments ago, you shuddered and woke,
Drawn for some reason into this scene.
But it's like trying to recall the instant
Your life was conceived. All you can see
Is snow falling on the still, white park,
Falling on the sculpted bronze flesh
Of some forgotten city father

Until even this solitary shape
Is nothing but white.

The Three-Bagger

Like clockwork, when the crickets began to chitter
And winds vacuumed the malt of humidity from the air,
My grandfather'd cart a stool from the kitchen
To the dark corner where the radio still squats.
He'd crouch low, cupping his deaf ear as if it hurt,
And would strain, in a trance, to hear
The perpendicular thwack
Of swung wood and rawhide connecting.

Just once, on a sandlot, before his twelfth birthday,
He cracked a corkball with a broomhandle so far
He forgot to run at first, it felt so good,
And still made a three-bagger, standing up.
The oldest of eight, he was drafted to fix
Sockets and wire lights before he saw his first curve
And so could only listen while his brothers
Broke in with clubs in the 3-I League,
And one of them, one summer, made it with Cleveland.

I imagine him still listening, even now,
Crouched upstairs above the vent in the wall.
On the mound in the basement with the count
Full, I lob the dog's ball, underhand,
To "Willie McGee," my four-year-old boy.
He becomes a transparent eyeball blending
His swing with the pitch—and as long
As the sound lasts—connecting us all.

A Splinter and a Flame

When a child is sick—
Your only begotten son,
His flesh a furnace kicking in
During a February blizzard—
Then, in the warm irregular puffs
Of the little boy's breathing, you feel
What luck it takes just to be born,
The single beached splinter of the nightly
Sinking of a thousand wrecked ships.
But you feel luckier still to have borne
This small-boned, delicate child this long,
To have kept him burning at all,
Like a wooden match flame in a hurricane.

Preheating

Midsummer, heat lingers like flannel in the dusk,
beading martini glasses with sweat. We touch
our drinks together, lightly, so they clink
like strangers at an airport grazing suitcases.

We forget the gas grill heating on the porch,
the squash and scallions simmering on the stove.
We only know desire, can only sense
the warmth that's waiting in the other's grasp.

Upstairs, like passengers, we don't look down
on what's below, coals glowing in the dark
like distant cities; nor to what awaits us—missed
connections, ruined food. Instead, we fly

into a banquet of flesh, blackening our bodies
on the grills of each other's bones, fillets
cooked fast on highest heat, but eaten slow.

Picnic in Iowa

If only we had known that when Manet
Began to paint *Le Déjeuner sur l'herbe,*
An idyll of soft light, breeze, shaded grass,
The wind hadn't breathed for three and a half days,
And the Seine River reeked, a dung-clogged barn.

If only we had known, as we drove through back roads
Bordering farms, watching glare make fence posts
Sweat and blacktop blister like peasants' feet,
Then we'd have kept the romance in the car—
The Pinot Noir, the Brie, the long-stemmed crystal.

Beyond barbed wire, the real thing:
Puddles of tar-black mud and mounds of brush,
The landscape of the long-married, who know,
As Manet knew, that fields like this are studios,
Messy beds, where art ends, and life begins.

The Gravity of Love

Ten years ago, at Heathrow Airport, our bodies
Touched, like the orbits of two planets coming
Together at last, guided since creation
By the gravity of love. Now we're apart.
You have your own space. But still, at night,
Above the dark that hides the dead trees
And the scarred fields upturned like graves,
The same stars shine light-years away.

November Dusk

Because last leaves have fallen, a new view
Blooms through the living room glass. The cold, gnarled
Branches of a sixty-year-old oak warm
Their knuckles in the glimmer of a light
Whose wax is gone. But the tree's freezing palms
Shine black, curved eastward like hands that have held
Death in dark, quiet rooms, hands that won't heal.
And though they'll never hold again the green
Coming of buds in early March, they'll stay
Open all winter, waving goodbye.

Shiftwork, in February, at Terre Haute Coke and Carbon

In winter, the cranes start eating
the mounds of black coke while it's still
dark out. On mornings so cold their numb tires
turn like blocks of ice, the smokestacks
cough up inky columns of snot and spit,
and the train tracks that vein the grounds
throb already under gauze strips of frost.
Even coal cars, empty at midnight, squat
hunchbacked with half-loads by the open docks.

Meanwhile, across the road, a small graveyard
glows in the refrigerated air. Tombstones
shine like typewriter keys used to punch out
the daily obits. But now, they're as white
with untouched snow as blank newsprint waiting
for someone to make a lasting impression.

In Memory of My Grandfather, William A. Brennan (1883-1972)

I have a photograph Dad took in 1957
of Pop and me sharing an armchair and showing
the same complacent, incipient smile—
as if he knew some secret and, without a single
syllable or motion, had impressed it on my mind.

I've never remembered posing for that picture,
parting my lips to inhale the breath he just sighed,
but engraved in time like Dürer woodcuts
are the stories he'd tell in Forest Park
where afternoon light would hit his face and hold,
for an instant, the gleam that gave his eyes their look.

Like the time installing spotlights in the dark dome
of the Arena ceiling, he lost footing and fell
off the scaffold, but having, that morning, shunned
suspenders for a thick cowhide belt, he was
caught by the buckle by his partner's free hand.

Or the time he boarded the train bound for Topeka
and got off to sleep in Boonville before moving on—
but feeling sick and restless checked out
and rode all the way home, where he read the next day
the hotel had burned down, everything reduced to ashes
so no one could tell one corpse from another.

On that last Thanksgiving, my first visit in two months,
he wore the same gay smile, lying
shriveled in the bedsheets like a leprechaun.
I see myself bending for the last press of his lips,
but I never saw him again, never
asked how to charge this etching with ink.

Stone Mountain

To the memory of Doug Johnson

At last, from your hometown, there is no motion.
On a crag jutting into shade, your right
boot just happened to graze ice whisking
you into the physics of falling snow.

Now, it has stopped falling; the wind
piling drifts by graves all afternoon, blows
somewhere else; and clouds, like gauze pads,
sop the wound of the quarter-moon.

There was such speed in your supple body
cleaving like a bronze rudder the blue lengths of the pool,
floodlights would sparkle in your wake like sharks.
But light moves faster in air than in water.

Come morning, sun will shine on Stone Mountain
as if nothing, nothing at all, has stopped.

Driving Home for Christmas

The interstate I'd seen a hundred times
in every season, from all angles of light,
lost its contours in vapor that poured
forty feet ahead in all directions.

It turned the landscape of woods and farms I knew
mile by mile into a land of unlikeness,
a land like the one in which my grandmother's mind
now lives: her past like pictures memorized

but now misplaced, and the present, an eye
that cannot shut, a road that will not end.

Forward

For Anita Coleman

Driving north on a back road in the twilight
Of April, the warmest day since last September
When a hard frost killed my black-thumbed marriage,
I watch the sun, like a sacrifice, bleed to death
Above green farms in eastern Indiana, in fields
Where life has just returned and nothing's ripe.

But still on the same road, I'm going
North from the broken lives that lie
Behind me, where day's already
Left, like a car hurtling
Forward from the dead body of a tire,
Its driver gripping the wheel

Like a lifeline she hopes will pull
Her from dark waters and into the air
Where light, if nothing else, will soon grow back.

From *The Sea-Crossing of Saint Brendan* | 2008

I. The Witness

One of fourteen

        our father had chosen

to sail the seas

        in search of the land

where Barrind the monk

        had made a visit,

I lock in memory

        these many months later

the looks of wonder

        in our man of the Word

as his soul envisaged

        a similar voyage;

and his satisfaction,

        his faith fulfilled,

when our craft cruised back

        into Brandon's Bay

and the towering cliffs

        west of Tralee

loomed so luminous

        with the light of sunset,

the monks all lining

        the top of the mount

and blessing the Lord

        for bringing back Brendan

and most of his men,

        monks like me.

We unloaded our gear

        and greeted our loved ones.

Then after the Mass

by dining together

Brendan broke silence,

which below I'll narrate

II. Barrind's Story

Seven years before

after Barrind came

his sensational report.

with a vivid desire,

to the Promised Land,

had just sailed off from,

blinded their approach,

radiated round them

of gardens and greenery,

and a river rushing

and breaking our fast

like Christ and his crew,

and started his story,

in our leader's name.

we set out to sea,

and broached to Brendan

The saint was pierced

vowed to voyage

where Barrind and his lad

where fog like snowfall

before blossoming light

a reality of splendor,

of fullness and fruit,

through a fertile ravine.

They dallied for forty

days and nights

but the sun never moved

and the men never slept.

Barrind finished,

"Someone stepped forward

from the celestial brightness

like a boat that breaches

the horizon at sunset

and said 'Head home

and announce the news

that Christ is the light.'"

Now Brendan's eyes widened

wondrously wakened;

he declared he'd leave

from his native land

to pursue the numinous

across the seas.

III. Building the Boat and Setting Sail

Using few tools

we contrived a vessel

ribbed and limbed

with timber from oaks

and fleshed with oxhides

tanned by tree bark.

We smeared the skin

with tallow and beeswax.

The mast in the middle—

was solid as stone.

to last till landing,

to rebuild the boat.

till the tide turned.

a high sky

and a circle of sunlight

Finally at sunset

we rowed from the creek

The light behind us,

brightened our cells

who waved good-bye.

and the sails grew full

our hand-made home

steering westward

a flax-covered cross—

We stowed a larder

and loaded supplies

We bided time

Morning had tainted

with white clouds

suffusing the mist.

before darkness fell

right into the swells.

like a heavenly halo,

and the band of brothers

We begged God's blessing

of the Holy Spirit;

heaved with the wind,

Our canvas glinted

while the cliffside slowly

and salt spray—

baptized our souls

IV. Sailing the Seas

For sixteen days

on bountiful winds,

as a glutton's gut.

were no longer needed

Our boat rode along

of gray-green waves

in our eyes and ears.

fell like fire

that glued sky to sea.

toward summer solstice.

with a golden glory

sank out of sight

a sanctified water—

so we felt re-born.

the sail feasted

bloated and taut

Our oars like forks

till the sails slackened.

the looping slopes

that whipped white spume

At evening, the sun

flaming the line

Its golden thread glowed

on the horizon's rim

Amid whitecaps and waves

and when the moon anchored

I'd nap on my back,

for wind and for rain

So day and night

low in the water

till the hull heaved up

the sloping seawater.

like teetering timber

cushioned the crash

Suddenly the doldrums

God willed the waves

The sea grew solemn,

like a monk at the altar

long after moonrise.

starlight was winking

like a kite in the sky

nervously bracing

to wrack our rest.

we navigated northward

so waves would loom

and rolled us over

The mast would squeak

but oxhide, like towels,

against the gunwale.

dropped upon us.

to wane and flatten.

still and quiet

We rowed and rowed

our sinews' numb

Our spirits drooped

but Brendan, our father,

"Don't be aghast

He's our helmsman and helper,

So store the oars

Thus Brendan emboldened

and swayed us to wait

until God's good will

in whatever realm

in a monastery chapel.

till our ribs nearly cracked,

and enervated.

depressed as the sails,

offered this foresight:

for God will guide us.

our heavenly rudder.

and stop all your worry."

his fourteen boatsmen

with wise passiveness

gave back the wind

we next must roam.

From *The House with the Mansard Roof* | 2009

The Past

To make it live, as Vermeer tried
for Arnolfini, approximates
how memory works, the texture of
the way things were. But what once flared—

a spot of time, vividly fixed
in the mind's permanent collection—
always fades, like the sun's rays
reflected from a pewter plate.

Take *Lake Calhoun*, a photograph,
1980. It shows a mist
obscuring the sun one fall morning
in Minnesota, but the print

itself is dim, and even though
the sunrise happened, something's lost
to the outer eye—so only feeling
for the fleeting light survives.

Night Piece in Cork

Unable to sleep at 3 a.m., I go
to the open window of my third-floor room,
looming high up on Military Hill.
Downtown unfolds beneath me like a quilt,
the river stitching this hillside to uplands
in the south. Farther off, beyond the darkness,
the river herring-bones into the sea.
Tonight, there is no light from stars for miles.

It makes me think of my own flesh and blood,
the brood that came from Tipperary
and County Cork, but now are gone and never
known by us. They must have trooped to town
on market days, before the first dawn light,
when stars were threads in the dark open skies,
furrows in fields that later led them home.

The lights that pulse in this too-quiet night
can't animate the dead and can't return
to Cork what shined in their long-ended lives.
But surely some illumination comes
from rooftops and lamps of Brennans listed still
in the Cork city phone book. Even now
I see the surface of the river glow,
a candle lit on All Souls' Day that flickers

until the wick burns out and its last light
changes to smoke, the way a river empties
into a bay, its water sewn into the sea.

Prohibition

In Ben Shahn's Depression mural, Feds force
foaming beer from sixteen-gallon kegs down
an open drain. It flushes through the city's sewers
and mixes with rainwatered muck that runs
into the river, whose black, viscous surface
suds at night like mugs of Guinness stout.

Ben Shahn leaves the rest untold: the Feds
lowering their fedoras' brims and sidling
from afternoon light into the dark booths
of some back-alley joint, its windows boarded,
its door unmarked like bottles they pass back
and forth. At home, my grandmother—divorced
and poor but lifelong loyalist of Hoover's ilk—
sips her last glass of bathtub gin, then makes

her first and final radical move: She'll throw
her vote to Roosevelt, and vows never again
to swill near-beer at Bevo Mill—but never
forgot those nights when, under stars, she danced
away her sober youth in the arms of men
with chests like beer barrels, empty and dark.

Eads Bridge, St. Louis, 1935

After *The Bridges*, a WPA print by John M. Foster

Under Eads Bridge, the homeless gathered
In shadows, like *staffage* in dimly lit
Dutch paintings. Mornings, they would watch
The waves for hours, their poles propped
From rocks, their lines sunk into
The sluicing, liquid mud where stray
Catfish could be caught—if good luck struck.

One Sunday in June, Grandfather, tired
From double shifts at City Hospital, embarked
On a patron's pleasure boat to cruise up
And down the brown, indifferent waters.
By two, the sun glared, boiling the thick soup
Of bouillabaisse that circled them, and burned
The metal deck and rails like spoons left on
A hot stove. He could take it no longer:

Stripped to his boxers, wiped his brow,
Then jumped, jackknifing into
The pliant muck. Immediately, cold currents
Rushed up to enfold his overheated flesh.
Eyes closed, he felt refreshed—but then uprising
To breathe in air again, he found a ring
Of turds about to hook around his neck
And instantly knew this down-and-out decade
Was not about to let him go.

Fall Plowing

After a WPA painting by Grant Wood, 1931

America's begun to go to bed hungry,
        but everywhere, in Iowa, the land
                looks tillable. The fields slope

and roll in forms palpable to the naked eye,
        which slides into Wood's imagined span
                like a lover's gentle hand. It first works over

a silken hip, then slowly curves inward
        to smooth some rows of folded flesh—
                until the gaze, uprising, abruptly empalms

two looming parabolic shapes, ground so
        green and round with hope it feeds you more
                the more you look. But these twin hills

resemble, too, a still-life's bowls, turned over
        and empty, like the flat, fruitless hands
                you hold back from the canvas.

The House with the Mansard Roof

The house behind us waits for better days.
It's been betrayed eight times since we moved in
ten years ago, but was built long before
the road was paved. The mansard roof, which rises
high above both homes flanking it, reflects
the past; the shingles shine like silver plates
in early morning light. The western walls

wear shingles too—but in the shade, they're jagged,
nubby meth teeth. Below, the back porch sags,
weighted down by decades of dead beats
who trash the place and then bolt, grinning through
a pick-up's greasy glass. The yard out back
becomes a mudslide when it rains. No matter who's
passed through, they've left a landfill of their lives,
furrows of beer cans, butts, and pissed-on chairs.

But now the furniture and crap are gone.
The windows—blocked with plywood boards—
keep out the light. And yet the inner rooms are rich
in darkness, like black earth beneath the sills,
where weeds with bride-white lace have taken root.

Granary Days

At dusk, when August haze would glow on corn
Like attic dust, we'd head for Edwardsville,
The Missouri sun behind us, blazing in
The liquid lap of the Mississippi. We'd
Have slaved since morning, painted clapboard dormers
From jerry-built platforms, or cut green lawns
In Ladue the size of outfields—all day
Waiting for night to come. And then, at last,
We went: rode by Cahokia Mounds, toward
The darkness, to the Granary Bar, its parking
Lot lights just turning on the moment we
Got there.
              Much later, at last call,
We'd leave, our ears and hearts ringing, our eyes
Beer-bleary and red from gawking, lovesick
With girls we'd never get. Homeward, the air
Flew through us like a salve, drugged us, blocked out
What only now I recognize:
Mist creeping up in darkness like regret,
Possibilities I couldn't get my arms
Around, not till now, now that it's too late,
The Granary bare, its doors boarded shut.

First Kiss

We'd hidden from the nuns behind a wooded lot
and let our lips slip into place, lubricious
pulped tongues about to touch. I felt a rush

of pleasure piqued by sin. It felt as though
we'd stolen into our neighbor's cellar
and pried into his stash of cobwebbed boxes—

postcards in French, pin-up girls, parts of guns—
while upstairs lumbering above us, he made
the floorboards sway, like treetops about to fall.

At Mercouri's Restaurant

                        Mornings, mist rose
off the cold water when the sun poured in,
lighting a path to shore where anchored boats
bobbed and strained. Mercouri'd stand among
the empty outdoor tables, staring at the waves
and yearning for the world he'd left behind.

                        One day at lunch
Hellas came to him: a boy not twelve
and Aphrodite, bronzed skin glimmering
against a top that gripped her torso tight.
She nibbled at some perch, sipped half a Tab,
then swiveled her long legs and tilted face

to meet his fish-eyed gaze head on—
but by the time he could advance she'd slipped
outside again into the blinding light.
He felt like swine that Circe had no itch for.
Among their plates he found a glass of water
overturned. Under it, the coins she'd touched

shining in clear view, but out of reach.

The Fair Oaks Apartments Revisited

I've come to see again the place
We spent our year as newlyweds.
Two decades and divorce erase
What drew us from our separate beds.

From a park bench across the street
The brick and windows seem the same
And the oaks out front complete
The picture giving it its name.

And yet the lives we lived inside
Belonged to other people, whom
I'd never recognize. I've tried
To bury that young bride and groom.

White gulls with black-tipped wings are wheeling
Overhead, criss-crossing west
To east and back. One pair is squealing
As if a crow couched in its nest.

Epiphanies

The December we met I buried my past.
I drove to a funeral on New Year's Eve
And watched fog peel back like molting skin.
My windshield cleared to a dark farm
Where white birds were nursing the upturned ground,
While above, black ones flew into the distance.

Much later that night, I saw you downtown,
Framed by French doors that opened as you stepped
Outside, arms letting go. As if gazed at
Through gauze, your dress shimmered red as pressed flesh.
It was then the light changed: I turned and passed
A darkened church, its north curb clear of cars—

Though round the block I saw its single square
Of light, whose flare carries even now chords
Of an organ impressed by lonely, passionate hands.

Merton in Love
June 1966

Two months ago, bedridden at St. Joe's,
My body numbed, my wracked back fixed, I woke
And met M's eyes: Love-struck? Had I a choice?
I dove into the waters, where each stroke
Plunged me into the greater depths. What's real
Is inmost. Since we "borrowed" Brother Jim's
Unlocked sedan, I've been reborn, can feel
In us the freedom of the woods that brims
Over every branch and naked root.
Though we'll get caught like sophomores, she'll linger
In the subsoil of my wild mind. I doubt
A lot, but not that each twig feels her fingers:
Love lives in solitude; M's touch has powers
The abbot can't ban—even in cold showers.

After the Sack of South Carolina: W. Gilmore Simms in Exile
Columbia, March 1865

The night of fire, the negroes, terrified,
Skulked into their huts, lay low in darkness,
While Yankees wolfed down whiskey, bottle
After bottle, dumping what they could not drink
Onto the flames that flared from twenty windows
On the Isaacs' block alone. Columbia
Is blackened boards and ashes, hardly far
Enough from Woodlands, which we've bolted from
To hide out during Sherman's march downstate.
The stragglers we've seen here ignited fears
We left behind.

                    Last week we learned our home,
Rebuilt from cinders just three years ago,
Had burned again—ten thousand books consumed
Like papers wrapped round fat cigars. The Northern
Generals denied their part; I'm shamed to say
At first I blamed the man they pointed to, the man
Their war is meant to save. Yet neighbors say
That Nimmons carried out my writing desk
And chair and watched his step so both were spared.

So now I cannot sleep, remembering
How Woodlands burned the first time: bright light pouring
From the sundered roof, tongues licking in
The upper rooms and halls—seconds until
A thousand bricks and boards
Let go when Nimmons ran a ladder up
And rescued me, who now has let him down.

Weekend Retreat in Brown County

Sunday, in oblique October light, we drive
Toward town, toward famous Main Street's

Knickknack boutiques. We pass trees
Dripping from night's hard rain, their blonde

Leaves glinting like beaten gold, and wind
Along a curvy creek, edging abrupt bends

And loops—when gravel grips us in a bottlenecked
S: before us, two deer staring like statues through

The glare of tinted windows. And then they
Enter a crack in the wild woods. Quickly

We park and walk across Beanblossom Bridge.
It lifts us over the teeming creek and leaves

Us amid crowding brush and canopies of pines,
Nine yards from where the buck and doe had vanished.

But now we've lost our path: We either turn
Back toward town, or improvise a way

To cut through the new growth, which long ago
Closed us out of the woods' darkness.

Leaving San Francisco Early

"... the dead ... reach us most easily just as we awaken."
—Saul Bellow, *Humboldt's Gift*

At four a.m., Pacific Heights is still,
Though your wife's in bed and aches for love
Already, pillow packed between her legs.

Random street lamps cut through the dark and stir
The sleeping mind like a tall cup of Peet's,
Steaming its dawn fog. This is the hour

The North Beach tide starts to slacken and makes
The quiet waves opaque. It's now in dreams
The dead come back, the ghosts we won't let in

Our thoughts once we're awake, on guard. But now
You're mesmerized by window squares of light
Whose shimmering refuses to harden under

The layered sheets of mist. You feel like
A ghost yourself, merging into the space
Between tall buildings, passing through a landscape

Luminous and strange and soon to disappear
When the stark light of morning wakes your wife
And returns the world of pressing, solid things.

On the Beara Peninsula

I sit here sipping a Sonoma Merlot
in southwest Ireland, taking in the view.

The sun has set the coast on fire, cresting
a hill of broken rocks and fuchsia hedges,

and Coulagh Bay's a luminous blue.
Beyond, the Atlantic tends to black,

so soon the fields will steep in night,
will mark what's missing, what is lost

beneath the starless sky on land
and sea. Yet out my window gnats

are basking in a golden haze hanging
in mid-air. So I do what can be done—

hold up my cup to the light, while the light lasts.

Adagio for Middle Age While Sitting Outside in Late October

The open window lets
Me hear, though muffled through the shade, the strings
  Play Barber's themes of last regrets
      And irrecoverable things.

The evening light can't compensate.
It fades beyond the neighbor's fence, which showers
  The yard with darkness, like a crate
      Overturned on flowers.

So now I'll take indoors
My present potted life. Inside the house,
  You walk across the hardwood floors
      Unbuttoning your blouse,

Where light—like that far past
The fence, but brighter—irradiates our room.
  Our candles burn down way too fast,
      But nip night's early bloom.

Regarding the Old Poets, after the Reading
For Donald Hall and W.D. Snodgrass

Lagging their hosts by fifty feet,
the great ones—bent by abundance,
laden like fruit trees in fall—
lug their bags of books, limping.

A pair of sapling pines has framed them
and fixes their forms where western light
ignites the path they pace along,
bathing them in brilliance—
                              I hold the glow
in mind, then turn away before
they shuffle into the parking lot
overripened with shadows.

Winter Landscape
After C. D. Friedrich's oil, 1811

In old age life's become a winter landscape.
The traveler has come so far, through snow
Above his shins, through drifts between his knees.

Like hammered rocks, his bones crack when he slams
The crutches down, then like a pendulum
Swings the weight of an antique clock across

The miles and miles of frozen swells and flats.
This unmapped land's as uncompliant as
The god he'd begged to save his pregnant wife.

But that's all past. In Friedrich's winter scene
The snow has nearly stopped; he rests against
A rock by intermeshing firs, which guard

Him from the mortal storm. But note he's holding
Up his blistered palm as if it oozed
Like Christ's. It's clear he soon will die, but not

Forsaken: Friedrich's put a crucifix
Amid the trees—as if within the mind
Of this old man—and makes this place

A sacred spot, like the steeples rising out
Of sight, in mist unveiling what has always
Been there, that's everywhere he goes.

Watching the Sun Set from the Mount St. Francis Cemetery

Late afternoon, I walk the Stations of
The Cross—12 wooden silhouettes embedded
Beneath bare trees in a secluded gully.

When I step foot again on level ground,
A band of glowing orange stretches across
The distant treetops to the west, and above

A range of clouds—almost maroon—soon shades
To black. Beside the two new heaps of earth
And hay, I find a limestone bench and watch

The sky. Here, I remember the hopeless hunt
For my grandparents' stones ten years ago.
The unkempt grounds—grown wild—consumed what marked

Their loss. It felt like death had come again.
But now, I feel at peace and wait beside
The recent plantings till, as white as slabs

Not yet inscribed, the winter stars return.

Memorial Field, 1973

I'm standing on a hill, high
Behind the batter's box, where my brother
Digs in, alive, his full-count tip
Tumbled from the catcher's web.

The stars are out, and in deep left
A new moon's rising, like the grapefruit
Change a guy named Grace threw me here
Three years ago. My father

Missed that game, the June that cancer
Ruled his skies. But now he's telling
Me how good he feels, his nights
Shining once again, like insects

Swarming in the August glow
Below us, which will not dim until
The game is over, my brother
Stunned by a roundhouse curve.

Turning Point in the European Theater

New Year's Day, '45, my father marched
With Patton's Army to the Western Front,
The weather cold as a meat-locker, raw
And threatening sleet. Next day, they watched as snow
Fell and fell and the Moselle River turned
To ice, while generals, far off, planned to push

Them across the Siegfried Line and into hills
Dark with Nazi snipers—and from there
To victory. Here Dad would later pose
By walls unraveling, their threads loose and frayed.
Behind him in the river, "Hitler's Bridge,"
One side already sunk in frigid waters.

But weeks before in France, Dad thought he'd freeze
While sleeping. Patton came to kick their butts
And boost the troops' morale: "My men can eat
Their belts," he growled. And: "Anyone who loots
I'll shoot." Yet, Dad had sneaked into a vacant
House, quickly grabbed two woolen quilts, then stepped

Outside—at once he'd pressed both shoulder blades
Against the doorless jamb and held his breath:
Not two arm-lengths away appeared a jeep
In back of which sat Patton, just then turning
His head when the jeep jerked right to avoid
Some ice, like a marksman, startled by flares,

Who lifts a hand off the gun to shade his eyes.

Illuminations

New Year's, my father got the word:
"Five months to live." Then cardinals
Came to our snow-glazed ash,
A blaze amid the bloodless drifts.
The next night we woke to thunder
Above the roof, and our room luminous
As a flood light under water.

Now May has bloomed Dad's back yard green
And the world from his old bay window
Brims with new light. It's now I realize
High in the oak above the house
A mourning dove has come, its singular coos
Consoling the empty sunlit rooms.

Reprise

A Saturday in June, the lawn is mown
and the late afternoon light makes the glass
of the storm door shine. Only it is between

me and a flash of memory: Brubeck playing,
my father's front door open; just-cut grass
glowing in the glare of forty years ago,

and him, like me, abruptly glad to be
alive, right now, as a new breeze blows through
the maple's greenest leaves and "Take Five" fills

the house, a lung in rhythm with the notes.

The Gargoyle in Our Backyard

"... only two patients are alive and free of tumor at the time of this
report, both 7 years after resection. ..."

—"Oat Cell Carcinoma of the Lung: A Review of 138 Cases."
Cancer 23.3 (1969)

Thirty years ago, my father made medical history:
Staved off the cancer storming in his lung,
A squall that had sunk everyone else on board
His boat, capsized in cold, uncharted waters.
Last year, dismantled off our coast, he foundered
For good. We planted what's left in our inland grove.

All day, today, the western sky wore black,
Widowed young by a sun buried too soon.
At five, the darkness drove east, then unleashed
The grief of straight-line winds that leveled
Our ancient elm as if it had no roots.
It crashed across the fence whose white boards

Flattened like broken teeth. But amid the split spar
And a thousand chips, the gargoyle stands intact.
It guards the bits of bone and ash shipwrecked
Beneath it, emboldened by what survives.

The Sublime

"The sun is god." —J. M. W. Turner

When Turner lay dying, his curtained bed
Butted against the shuttered glass, he saw
Light landing on the window ledge like rain—
Just out of reach. His dry, paint-splotched hand opened
To hold the golden glow. He closed his eyes.

He dreamed of barges and freighters docked.
Leftward, a row of domes, smokestacks, and spires.
Rightward, a vacant pier that juts into
A bay of haze and black waters—and all
On fire from blotches burning far beyond

Toward which the ship in the center moves and grasps
For something to tug it from the coming darkness.

From *One Life* | 2016

Views from Union Hospital, New Year's

A day of gray, unspoken thoughts. And yet,
I saw the sun rise over snowy fields
beyond the lot, just as we parked the car.
The brilliant glimmer made me pause, and I
felt, for a second, anchored to the earth.

Later, installed in my third-story room,
I watched the western sky—above a block
of shabby, clapboard shacks and feet of snow—
fade from a bloody stain to black. The patient
beyond our common curtain slept, or died.

But soon they moved me to a floor below,
facing northeast. I did not dream that night—
oblivious to light and dark, to time,
to what's to come—and then I woke, my eyes
angling along the rows of trees that led

toward home, in the still-dim, invisible distance.

Epiphany

The end of summer, on the Wabash River:
The day began like a hundred others,
Hot as Oklahoma. The country roads—
Just ruts and rocks—felt like streambeds of dust,
And the river looked as stagnant as a sewer.
We went to the picnic as a point of duty.
Potluck, chitchat—we'd leave by six.

But as dusk fell, a breeze blew in. A neighbor
Untied his boat from pylons, and blue sky
Slipped down in the east, turning to maroon
Above the willows and the sycamores.
We climbed aboard and watched the bank flare up
Like campfire. Skirting a sandbar, we moved
Upstream. The rudder caught a current, curved
Slowly around a bend—when a heron swooped
And rose, hurling its wings outward and whisking
Past the last landing and into a wild woods.

With Durkee's dock behind us, just the dark
Ahead, a blur of ghost-white Asian carp
Cartwheeled into the air, their arc
A spotlight in the coming night, then dropped

Down under water—and into our dreams.

Yard Sale

"There is no object so foul that intense light will not make beautiful."

—Emerson, *Nature*

The renters bring out their greasy table,
End of the month again. It sags,
Weighted and warped like them, unable
To hold much more than glasses and rags.

Old clothes and rusty tools compete
For space with magazines they stole
From garbage bins behind our street.
Each shoe reveals a run-down sole.

A few come by, inspect, and leave,
Almost always with empty hands.
But when, at sundown, all things cleave
To slanted light, and when it lands

So rubber, glass, and metal glint—
And for a moment make you squint—
You'll see our neighbors bathed in gold
As if their worth cannot be sold.

One Life

Once more, the aftermath: Last week a line
Of winds leveled our town, clear-cutting trees
As old as Vigo County's oldest home.
Before, we'd lost a dying, bark-scarred oak.
Our other trees still stand. Amid the whirr and buzz
Of saws and chippers everywhere around
Us, Daphne and Apollo—purple ash and poplar—
Stir in the breeze, but stay unflappable.

Their branches arch above me like a nave
And now a silence spreads about. The wind
Animates the higher limbs, lifts them
Enough to let a slant of light slip through
Their folded hands and land on each green leaf
And me, the trees translucent as stained glass.

Awakening Next to an Open Window

The first cool morning of September floods
our sleep, like rain suddenly drowning ground
as dry as gravel. Overnight the August
heat heaved up its dust-laden boots and beat
it farther south. So now the sky is gray,
the clouds a watercolor seascape, wet
to touch, and high in the highest of treetops
the mourning doves sound out the shore of fall.

Home Movie

I'm seven, eye-patched and brandishing
a rubber knife while my mother waits,
cake-cutter in hand, for me to blow
the eight candles out. I'm antsy
and can't sit still, but fill with air.

She is dark-haired again, blue eyes
blinded by the sun-gun's glare
but shining; her teeth glow white
as crossbones on a pirate's flag
when it meets the morning light.

I remember so vividly how
the tiny flames flashed
in both our faces I now forget
what's next: her fleeting touch on my little
arm, my chance to empty out my lungs

and make the burning moment vanish.

Remembering the River
For my brothers

Easter weekend—we'd decamped
for the Ozarks, east of Joplin.
The Current River, almost flooding

its banks, bounced us across
cascading rocks and whitecaps
that foamed like wild dogs, but kept us

afloat and led our little fleet
downstream, as if tethered to a leash,
until we rested on still waters.

Silent as sleep for thirty years,
their memory lay in wait, but wakes me now,
making the mad rapids rise again.

The Tigris River

1.
(1258, Mesopotamia)
As the full moon is setting and the sky
whitens with dawn, a line of Mongols stands,
still as the night that's dying, on the edge
of waters, waiting. Then Khan's grandson lifts
his blazing torch and day begins: His hordes,
heaving themselves across the river, rage
into the heart of Baghdad burning all
that's in their way—the market, gardens, barns,
and bodies. Stragglers carting stacks of books,
armful on armful, to the Tigris
dump them in and turn the water black.

2.
(2003, Iraq)
Baghdad, in April—weather never better,
the morning calm, the Tigris gilt with light;
the coalition army guarding oil
in fields so vast that they look just like Texas.
Fort Jackson's troops, like statues, never move
all day and stay inside their bureau. Even
when flames fly up a hundred feet into
the sky, three miles away. And even when
they see a man, a Brit named Fisk, sprint toward
them, waving both arms, screaming that a mob
has charged like fire into the Library, looting
the ancient legacies of Babylon,
Sumeria, and the cradle of the world.
It burns the building down, and so the oldest
Qur'an, begun a thousand years ago, is ash.
Nearby, the Tigris River, washed in light,
runs its relentless waters toward the sea.

The Summer of Love

I was twelve. Fields of sleep and splendor sealed
me in a world just born and blooming. Flower
Power, in San Francisco, turned on hippies
at Haight and Ashbury, drugged on Ginsberg's mantras.
Deadheads who danced and jazzed for love had visions
fed by acid while Coyote fed
the hungry Diggers' dinners in the streets,
Quicksilver's music coursing through the air.

I tuned into KXOK, grew hair
over my ears, and fell in love, dreamed dreams
of lovely Sally, leggy, blonde, and hot
for me. The mere idea made me high
and all that summer of love-ins, I lived
in my head, heady, happy, never kissed.

Hazlitt in Love

Parted from my spouse, my marriage dead,
I found new life within a boarding house.
The tailor's daughter knocked, then filled the frame
Like Titian's Venus. The teapot she'd touched
Gleamed after she was gone, and as she left
She paused, turned fully round, then ran her eyes
Right through me—"Is he caught?" she thought. I was,
And am. That brazen gaze has made me mad.

I cannot work—all things in nature, art,
The dingy streets call up her face and trace
The circle of her waist. Though friends may think
Her eyes are slimy like a snake's and others
She's bony like scrag-ends of mutton chops,
I'm bit. I've lipped her as she strode my lap.

19 York Street
(Home to Hazlitt, tenant of utilitarian Jeremy Bentham; earlier, home to Milton)

The night I sat in back at Covent Garden
to watch John Milton's *Comus*, my landlord
Bentham evicted me from Milton's home.
Last year he bricked the yard where the blind bard
wrote his masterpiece—beneath an oak
uprooted when the fence was moved. I hear
the man now plans to do a favor for
a Miltonist in the Middle West who wants
a souvenir: rip out the staircase, board
by board, then ship it all across the sea
in a hold crammed with whisky, tea, and rats.
I think of when the church was fixed, John's grave
dug up and open. Scoundrels knocked out teeth,
grabbed bones and fists of hair and hauled them off
to sell in a dark mews or smelly pub.

Now rootless, too, booted like Adam, but
without my Eve, I wind my solitary
way from the Eden of my mind. And yet,
beneath the window facing the old garden,
I leave behind a stone to mark what's gone.
The few—who make up for "the greatest number"—
can imagine Milton in this space
and keep his chiseled name from being lost.

Termites

Now that you're gone, the termites have come,
their mud trails lining the bedroom wall like cracks
in plaster. I sponge the topsoil up: out of sight,

out of mind—almost. Today, what's been rotting
out my inner core swarms up

from a pipe beneath the bathroom sink—
a place I'd never looked before—then spreads
across the tiled floor, where, like fallen

angels, they drop their diaphanous wings,
as if they no longer have the heart to fly.

July in Indiana

Saturday—I wake at dawn
to winds whirling in swollen skies
and drying dew that's layered on
our lawn too brown to fertilize.
For days the sun has burned and boiled.
For weeks, we've sweated through the nights
so sultry even feet recoiled
from flesh, afraid we might unite.

But something stirs within the room,
and within me. Cold air outside
flows in, embedding your perfume
amid the swirling breeze. What died
in sheets we kicked off hours ago
springs up like a tulip in the snow.

Jam Session

After Fred Becker's print, 1937

In the woodcut, the black-and-white quintet
moves with the music—their wrinkled coat-sleeves,
the creases crossing their foreheads in waves;
even their fingers sing, gyrating joy.

I hear the notes of "West End Blues," a tune
my grandfather played in London, near
Bloomsbury and Southampton Row,
in nineteen-twenty-six. I see this scene:

Outside the Cora Inn, where black cabs park,
flappers and their beaux march two by two
and pigeons circumvent the square, their feathers
blending with ashen clouds about to salt
the night with snow—a harbinger
of things to come.
                        But in the bar he's blind
to markets and war, and the cold, dawn walk back
is hours away. He's cooking at the keyboard,
the quicksilver sound surrounding him
soon to be quiet as a spot of time.

Le Grande Perch de Terre Haute

After a print by David Erickson, 2007

Leaving the ripened fields of wheat
before the early snow,
the cawing crows arrive in crowds—
a painting by Van Gogh.

At dusk, across the Wabash River,
a yellow light remains,
while swirling birds as black as ink
darken the sky like stains,

then pack the leafless trees like pews,
parishioners in a church.
One, higher than the rest, has made
the courthouse dome his perch.

Burlesque

After Mabel Dwight's lithograph, c. 1935

The gentlemen pack the hall
On Monday afternoons.
Their eyes are lights in darkness,
Their grins are quarter-moons.

They've put all calls on hold
Since sales are so few.
They've left behind their ledgers
And sample cases, too.

It's as if they're on an island,
For now they're mesmerized
By the *femmes* they feast on
And no one is surprised

That hunger keeps increasing
As the girls leg out the jigs,
Their teeth like strings of pearls
Thrown in front of pigs.

Land of Plenty
After Lucienne Bloch's print, 1935

The vagrants trudging through the muddy ruts
have printed black. Their lives are now
just blots of darkness, their frayed hems
jagged as glass, their humanity flattened.
They bend to the times, but lean ahead.
They're looking for something beyond
the border of the woodcut's frame.

To their left, barbed-wire blocks them from
the looming middle distance. Corn stalks brim
over to the foreground, like a crowd
crushing into a busy street. It pushes
the family almost off the bottom of
the picture space. Only the boy has turned
to look—but he can't see the power lines

that scrape the sky and bring light somewhere else.

La Cuisine des Beaux Arts

Thanksgiving—early light's all haze and grays,
But comes in through the window by the sink.
Robed and unwashed, the risen cook arrays
The tools of his trade, then stirs a drink,

A gin martini with a twist. Inspired,
He takes the turkey from the fridge. It thawed
Overnight and marinated, mired
In spices and a sauce Prudhomme would laud.

In the stove, heated at three-twenty-five,
The bird will warm, a canvas left to dry,
While the chef preps a palette of some chive
And oil, like Turner touching up his sky
Before the opening at noon. Then food and wine—
The gourmet's art—will please the taste of all as fine.

The Ballad of General William Westmoreland (Ret.)

Although my hair's above the ears
And though it's growing gray,
Unwittingly my knee-long shorts
And naked legs betray

A hairy rebel's attitude.
Or so the general thinks.
My plate of buffet food in hand,
I go to get our drinks,

But then the hostess intervenes,
A human barricade,
Demands I don a navy blazer,
And says that "I'm afraid

You can't get up again or you'll
Make the general mad."
More than thirty years before
Not yet an undergrad,

I watched my elder Boomers protest
The war Westmoreland waged,
Fitting flowers into rifles
And making guards enraged.

And now as if I'd dodged the draft
And fled to Montreal,
I've pricked the old man's thinnest skin
Not trying to at all.

But as we leave and pass his table,
Though I say not a word,
The body language of my legs
Flips the prig the bird.

Evening Shadows

The autumn you were twelve we played our last
game of wiffle ball in the old yard.
Oaks arched above us like a dome, while yews—
our warning track—straddled the fence we aimed for.

At the plate, I gripped the plastic bat to turn
on your three-fingered, crooked curve. As pitcher,
you'd stand where Cobb once stood against the Cubs,
his reach in center like a rake's that cleaned

the lawn of falling hits. That park is gone
and we do not belong here now. And yet
the moment—when your pitch, my swing connected—

hovers amid the leaves about to fall,
a shimmering blur within the shadows.

Quincey
In memoriam, 1996-2007

No feline so fine as the furball
        Find at Petco, a Persian that purred
Upon a single finger's touch. A mural
        Might match his beautiful fluff, but no mere word.

Two pictures tell: The fall Quincey's three,
        Sleeping on the couch. October air
Blows in, riffling the pages of poetry
        I'm reading, the moment it flutters his fur.

And this: I sit at my desk across
        From the sill that fills with Quincey, who's
Been watching since noon both the world outside us
        And one within, as if waiting on his muse.

Independence Day
In memory of my Mother

All afternoon, the clouds have painted the sky
the color of the gloss we'd bought to stain
our stuccoed porch. We'd wanted to apply
a coat or two by five o'clock, but rain

sloped down and soaked our block's houses, washing
over the rooftops, trees, and cars—a brush
loaded with black. The sounds of traffic sloshing
through the inky pools on Maple Road, the lush

dark leaves pending above, stirred up again
Suzanne's last Fourth of July. She would die
later that week. But till the rains began
that forced her from the porch, she watched the sky

where rockets were transmogrified, aware
they'd left their skins and vanished into air.

Remains
In memory of my Father

We've opened the house, pulled
Back dusty drapes left closed since Mother's death
A decade ago. You lived so long with
    No one here, growing old

    In artificial air
With no lights on, it's hard to know just how
You spent your days, what kept your spirits low
    And kept you in your chair.

    Some nights when you called me
I could almost smell the sweet vermouth
You'd stirred into your scotch to make your fourth
    Or fifth manhattan. We

    Never said much then,
But you were reaching to me from the dark
Side of your mind, where you'd repressed Sierck,
    France, and the German men

    Who made you who you are—
We think. You never talked to us about
The towns and battlefields, much less the route
    That led to your Bronze Star.

    At seventy, the river
You'd dammed inside since '45 broke through
At last: You wept and wept for the dead you knew,
    Forced to stay young forever

    While you lived fifty years
More. But in the end when we circled round
You, your face lit up as if now you'd found
    Just how to loose your fears.

So we'll take on your pains,
It being time for us to free you from
The dark. We step outside, then scoop up some
    Of the chalk-white remains

    Of what you were and are.
We sprinkle them beneath the maple tree
You planted when we first moved in—when we
    Had hearts without a scar.

Afterlife

1

Christmas, six months since Mother died. We leave
her grave, still green from the late fall, to hunt
for Dad's dead parents buried long ago.
We have a map but their stones, sunken under
the slowly sliding hill—its soil a glacial
avalanche—have vanished with their lives.
Then Dad blurts out, "They're here." But as I hurry
to cross the meadow, something makes me stop.
An upright slab of limestone: "Jerome Simon."
My mother's father. Whom we never knew.

2

No one now alive remembers you.
At Christmas dinner, though, I tell a few
of your contemporaries my good news.
The table, laid with silver, gilt-rimmed plates,
and crystal dishes, glitters like the tree—
until I blunder to your ex, my grandmother:
"We ran across Mom's father's grave today."
She blanches, grunting like I'd punched her gut;
breathless, without a word, she turns away.

Later, Aunt Betty laughs at what I've done.
"Oh, Louise. Many nights she rang our bell,
holding your mother's hand, and hot with tears
said Jerry'd gotten drunk again. Such drama.
She even claimed he beat her. What a queen."
I bite my tongue, but feel Grandmother's pain.

3

I learned of you when I was ten. Your picture
hung far above the basement stairs, almost
in darkness. Mom believed that you looked handsome,
dark-haired and dashing, and was proud of you,
appointed judge of city court at forty;
she next confessed your sins, your drive to drink

that plastered your fine face on the front pages
for cruising drunk. Divorced, you took the kids
a couple times to Sunday matinées.
And then no more. You drove them home, too stewed
to keep the Packard's wheels straight, swerving side
to side, steering with only knees and elbows,
peering ahead as if into a blizzard.

Your void filled fast and though the landlord's name
was yours—uncannily *Jerome I. Simon*,
a surgeon-jazz pianist—he lit up
rooms, sparking warmth in all he met and flames
in females like your ex, whose love for him,
a chandelier, now shined upon your kids
and gave their tarnished lives a sheen again.
Some nights, you'd park across the street and stare
up at the windows till the lights went out.
Your winter never ended, ice-cube cold
night-in, night-out, and so you moved backed home,
great promise emptied into greater drink.

4
The visits, then, were scarce, Sunday night dinner
your Irish mother made (and supervised).
Then years rolled by, the shadows round you grew
and kept you in the wings, off your kids' stage—
until your dad, in bed with a bad heart,
broke from the script. Scrambling your eggs,
you heard a boom, then bounded up the stairs
in terror. A snub-nose revolver lay
where once your head had nestled. So again
you made the paper, witness to a suicide.

5
The war years left you all alone, in exile,
dead-center where you started from. Out West,
my mom and aunt together studied at
UCLA; their house was on a base
(my grandpa ran the surgery, then later,

overseas, built a hospital to mend
Marines butchered and bombed by Japanese.)
They dated sailors, one a Yankee pitcher,
and hobnobbed with celebs—like Robert Taylor
and Joe E. Brown—even Van Johnson pulled
up his cock-red coupe to a Westwood curb
and tried to pick up Mom. Meanwhile, in Belgium,
Jerry Junior battled at the Bulge.
He lived, just like your younger stateside daughters.

6
But you did not. Amid parades and plans,
the post-war weddings, yet unwritten chapters,
your plot's become a folded page, a shadow
draft of the story, darkness on a hill.
You've missed our lives, just as you missed your own.
When I imagine you, you're only eighteen,
stranded by the Great War's grand armistice,
and waiting to ship out for Flanders Fields:
You stand on deck, dry-docked, gazing into
a harbor of haze, blind to what's beyond
this gateway to the future's other worlds.

View of Lake Louise
In memory of bartender Mike Timmons (1956-2011)

Few knew you had an artist's eye for light
And dark. For instance, in your great late photo
Of Lake Louise, we see sublimity:
Your camera frames a perfect square bisected
Width-wise—the lower showing turquoise water,
The top, the milky glacier and ghost-white
Sky rising from the fields of ice into
The cold, blank space the distance holds.
This beauty caught in Canada stayed out of mind
The tragic night you left the lens cap on.

I now remember when my wife and I
Steered our boat, like you, on Lake Louise
To where you glimpsed your visionary gleam.
The surface of the lake, fed by the glacier,
Was beautiful, but if you put your hand
Beneath the water, it would disappear.

The Hofbräuhaus

In Copenhagen once, my mother's parents
Boarded a boat about to heave into
The Baltic Sea, thousands of miles from home.
Yet the first faces they would see belonged
To next-door neighbors George and Gertrude Strong,
And neither couple knew the other'd left.

From Denmark—Nanny wrote down in a log—
They'd made their way to München. Bev and I
Were there, four decades later. Everyone
We met was strange, though often "picturesque."
At Hofbräuhaus, while men in lederhosen
Played the same tunes they played in 'sixty-two
And buxom blondes in low-cut dirndls dipped
And danced their way to tables, balancing
Beer mugs—as massive as their boobs—on trays
Crammed with plates of brats and sauerkraut,
We soaked it in, but left our steins half empty.

Last year, I found my grandma's souvenirs,
And in the only photo in her book,
They sit—our age, it looks, and where we sat—
Gazing into the lens as if at us,
As if to welcome us to Germany,
Raising their mugs up high, and brimming to the full.

The Nightingales

It was after midnight when our driver found
the Alfa Pension on the outskirts
of Wien, still later when he roused from sleep
an ancient innkeeper, who seemed jet-lagged
himself. We entered beneath the one dim bulb
shimmering through the darkness, a headlight
in fog. The innkeeper, dumb and muttering
German under his breath, gestured toward
the pitch-black hall, where we would find our room.

It was bare-bones: twin beds; a cordless phone,
which did not work; and a window opening
to wild, impenetrable, tangled woods.
I lay awake, but soon the April air
concussed, a choir of altos skirmishing
around a low, sweet bass, a sound that made
up for the moonless dark and harmonized
the blindness of the landscape with my dreams,
which rose within me like the Alps I'd yet to see.

In Bed at the Churchill Hotel, Ambleside

Our window reached from the wainscot to the top
Of the west-facing wall. Its view unveiled
Loughrigg Fell looming over us and clouds
That rested on the mountain like a spread.
We'd hiked the trails up to the ridge that rises
Ramp-like and rims a field full of sheep
Weathered as ancient stones. We'd even crossed
A running creek to gain the point of vision
Looking down on the tarn and, lower still,
The Elderwater lake. But now we saw
Just the peak, forgot the rugged rocks,
The mud, the loss of breath. So when you rolled
Over and the robe snowcapping your breasts
Fell open, I rose to a yet greater height.

A Fall Retreat on the Beara Peninsula

Each night at two I wake and hear rain rapping
The windows and the roof, as if to clean
My dreams and make me see again. At dawn,
All is fog that shrouds the meadows, homes,
And headlands far away as Coulagh Bay.

Today, by noon, the sun burned off the mist.
At five, I take a sloping road and pass
The houses made of local stones, their hedges
Of fuchsia not yet bloomed—to where the path
Opens to a view of seagulls, boats,
And rolling ocean waves. But it's a vision
For a postcard. I look a while, then wind
My way downhill, eyes earthward, blind and deaf
In the silent dusk that's coming on—until

Within, beneath, beyond the bounding hedges
I hear an inland murmur, water running
Underground, the undersound I'd slept through.

Manet Painting in Monet's Garden, 1874

Now, after seeing *Garden of the Princess* years ago
through a plate-glass window and wincing at
Monet's disdain for paintings made indoors,
I've stepped outside myself into the light.

When Claude came back from Britain, I found
him a house in Argenteuil, and he found
his bliss—a garden, bottles of Bordeaux,
a rowboat to paint from on the Seine.

"Monet is just an eye," Cézanne once said,
"but what an eye." That summer, Monet's eye
captured lights no eye'd ever seen: All forms
dissolved in flickering visions in the open air.

He painted "as a skylark sings," suffused
in daylight's luminescence. A flurry
of brushstrokes, small and swift as Camille's lashes,
enveloped first impressions on forty canvasses.

So I left the shadows of my studio, landing on
the riverbank where Claude, in curving jabs
of broken color, caught the water's luminous blues.
I walked into the true light of nature.

One Sunday afternoon, I went to Monet's garden.
I took my brush and canvas out of doors
and amid the scintillating lilies, Camille sprawling
in linen on the June-green grass, I felt

the impress of something vibrant but ephemeral
and suddenly began to paint in a new light.

Walking Man

Each morning, while I walk on the treadmill
Centered before a second-story window,
A lanky man, late sixties, ambles by
Along the street. His swinging arms keep pace
In rhythm with his moving feet; his eyes
Stay fixed on something just ahead, a future
He almost sees, but it's a mystery.
Again today he saunters by as always,
Inward, subdued, at one with the sidewalk,
The wind, the morning light that gleams behind him.
Once he's out of view, I look beyond
The leafless trees into a front of clouds.

Beethoven's *Fifth* shudders through my earphones
And I remember reading of John Dwight,
A Transcendentalist who'd walk long miles
Round trip to Boston from Brook Farm to hear
The first four notes—they filled his mind with strangeness
And led him, passing by the wind-thrashed trees,
To feel a dark foreboding in the night
And a nameless exultation too.
Just so, when my old life foundered, I walked
The lonely, moonlit streets for hours, this wild,
Uncontainable surge within, a wedding
Of fear and longing, and yearned for the stars
Drifting away into the shipwrecked night.

But walking man is quiet, even-keeled,
And calm; he takes the measure of the world
In ordered, stoic, meditative steps—
One who has lived through thunderstorms of grief,
Trekking dark passages, and who now seeks
The power underlying solitude.

New Poems |

Spring in Town

It snowed again on Sunday night. We heard
the furnace kick and groan like an old man
sleeping, but gripped in great, bone-wracking pain.
A winding sheet of ice wrapped round the roof.

Today, the sun is brushing the blue sky
with blush and fresh foundation, and a row
of golden daffodils spangles a lawn.
The same light's bronzing the long spines of trees.

She's fashionably late, but spring is coming.
She'll soon rip through the threadbare coat of winter,
and will strut down the runway wearing feathers
bolder than the old man's ever dreamed of.

At the Esterházy Palace, Twilight

From my courtyard bench, I strain to hear
the quartet playing in the Haydnsaal,
its harmonies and haltings, its struck strings
falling, then rising like a fountain's stream.
But now this music mingles with another
orchestration—the scrapes and scrubs of masons
remaking the North Tower's ancient walls.
I marvel at their labor, sweat that serves
Beauty, too. So, I wait until their racket
rings no more, and the cello's sweet, sad notes
surge up like waves beneath the waxing moon,
muffling the workmen's stuccoed craftsmanship.

Late Fall, Leaving Terre Haute on Highway 40

During the dogs days of August
Thirty years ago, I drove
To my new home, gazing through heat
And haze at the blurry summer crops,
Then breathed the dirty urban air.

After nightfall on the shabby streets,
Moonlight like rain would rinse the city.
And season by season it started to fit
Like old, weather-beaten shoes
That shape your life into their image.

But now I feel the urge to molt:
Past the downtown bridge, the river
Widens, its wetlands pooling where
The winter crows will come, then wing
Their dark way across the waters.

Winter Solstice, Sunrise

I dreamed last night I'd really died.
The car I'm in bypassed a bridge,
broke through a fence, and hurtled
airborne over a gulley's ridge.

I woke up sweating and almost swore
my soul had swooned, in flight to where
I'll pass eternity. My mind
grew dark, and I gasped for air.

But now I look around our room—
a bathrobe hanging on a hook,
the photo from our wedding day,
the bedside table and an open book.

Suddenly, I'm flooded with new intentions:
"I'm here," and light as my pillow's feathers.
The window frames a cold, brisk morning,
the coming months of winter weather,

but sunshine drives the shadows back,
dousing everything in sight—
traffic, children, guardrails, houses—
with a warm, baptismal light.

Midtown, in Midwinter

Tonight the moon is lighting up the sky.
Bits of stars prick through the scrim of clouds
And glimmer like streetlamps six blocks away.

But here the bulbs are burnt out, so the neighbors'
front lawn is dark; a rusty cart from Save-A-Lot

is stuck in dirty snow, and the pin oaks
extend their scraggly branches high into
the air, reaching for light. Meanwhile, in bed,

the tenants grind their teeth, dreaming of grit,
darkness on guard outside their broken windows.

The Widow in Winter

Every spring, in closets planked with cedar,
our grandmother would zipper mothballs into
garment bags to sheath her winter clothes,
now out-of-season, till the first frost comes.
Somehow the mothballs' scent enveloped all
the rooms and lingers in my memory still:
I see her sitting in the breakfast nook—
back ramrod straight, Virginia Slims in hand—

and living once again the autumn nights
when the Jazz Age began and just eighteen,
a freshman at a D.C. boarding school,
she stole outside her dorm to smoke, coatless,
but fashioning herself to brave
the changing weather, and to wear it well.

Old Bottles

What wastes young flesh and makes it old
before its time? It doesn't age like wine,

stored cold and deep in darkness underground
and waiting patiently for lips to part

anticipating consummation. Neither
is our carcass an old bottle keeping

all it holds preserved in sweet delay.
Early, it pops its cork; its contents spill

or sour or simply vaporize. Still, sometimes
we turn our empty bottles into lamps

that keep the brand of memory burning.

Tipperary

At the guest house, they hadn't heard of Loughmore,
the parish where my grandfather's old man
was born and baptized during the Great Hunger.

Ryans and O'Neills on every road—
dry cleaning, diners, butchers, bakeries, pubs—
their names emblazoned everywhere, but ours

nowhere in sight. Our hostess led us back
behind the lodge and down a lane her family
owned when Cromwell wrecked the countryside.

Still standing, a stone home no bigger than
a shed that peasants had lived in from birth
to death. Burn marks blackened the bricks

that once made up a hearth. No window cracked.
But the thatch roof was rent and let in light
that filled the space, like breath inhaled.

My Father's Coat

Some days I wear my father's Donegal tweed,
though the silk lining's torn and buttons sport
unraveling threads. He wore it the cold morning
we walked across the quad, surrounded by
the stately limestone halls and Doric columns.

Two backpacked students passed and when one said
hello, my father grinned, flattered they thought
he was the dean, he who had lined our walls
with novels—Faulkner, Maugham, Fitzgerald, Joyce—
the Great Books too, their weight warping the boards,
their substance loosening screws and brackets.

When he was dying, gripped with second thoughts,
he mourned the open doors he never entered.
So when I walk into my morning class
on days I'm clothed in tweed, I'm not alone,
the frayed threads linking me to what the coat's outlived.

The Minneapolis Years

After thirty years, today I've gone
down dusty stairs into the basement, brushed
off sticky spider webs, then folded open
my boxed-up past. A cache of photographs
evokes another world before divorce—
our bungalow just north of Lake Nokomis.

I turn an album's pages, lost years passing
into forgetfulness, and floating motes
rise up, the particles of buried memories
I molted like old skin we never miss.

But now I lift a picture of my son
when he was five, a smiling birthday boy
who's staring back at me, and like the man
beside him—me, but not so old—I want
to hold his hand, as if to keep him there.

Two Views of San Francisco

1

Last time we came here, the fourth floor revealed
a view commensurate to the wine I drank.
The high sky shed its clouds, as if exposing
skin as soft as glossy Chinese silk.
Before our eyes, a seagull glided building
to building in great windswept surges destined
for the bay. We watched a woman on a rooftop
walk around watching the same bird begin
to merge into the cool but luminous air.

2

This time we are not here to see the sights.
Your fading vision needs an optic fix;
a tricky laser surgery has brought
us back. Your blurry world is closing in,
fog blotting out the high-rise lofts across
Van Ness and whiting out the next blocks' hills.
All's sober now, like boats tied up in harbor.
We wait to see if afternoon burns off
the fog, brings back the firmament into view.

A Re-Vision

I step out of the lot of blowing snow
and enter Subway when it's packed at noon.
At the counter no one's ordering.
I overlook a shape conversing with
the girl at the register. It's just
white noise to me. I want my wheat bread toasted
and only a short squirt of mustard on
the peppers topping my meat.
                              It is now
that I turn toward the figure waiting for
change and find a man I knew who'd moved
away ten years ago. I'd thought he died
and I would never lay sore eyes on him,
who once invited me to come and swim
in his pool, but—it turned out—just to sell
us his ramshackle ranch for more than it
was worth. His students bitched—and they were right—
that he was "shit with feet."
                              And yet I'm thrilled
to see him once again. I blurt out, "Bill"—
as if my plane went down amid the timbers,
but I had made my snowblind way back home
and he was the first soul to welcome me.

The Biocaust across the Street

What had been rolling fields rooted with brush
and trees three hundred years old—some of which
shaded our sidewalk on the eastern edge
of Preserve Creek—is now a bulldozed span
of dirt. Each day, earthmovers and dumptrucks,
steamrollers, backhoes, graders, cranes, shift
the ground around, whirling dustbowls like smoke
that clouds a bombed-out town. A constant din
of grinding gears and metal parts concusses
like tanks clanking along the River Somme.

The last to flee were geese, though mourning doves
have stopped on rooftops singing sad laments
for what is gone and won't be coming back.
And though the hornfrogs left and countless birds
have perished or moved on, their nests wiped out,
today I saw a fawn escape into
a stand of oaks still dark with summer growth
and greenery that lets a person breathe.

Late Summer, Strolling by a Neighbor's Garden

I notice that her bleeding hearts, whose blooms
uplifted us in May, have now been long
dried out like petals pressed in heavy books.
And where I walk, the pavement—rinsed by rain—
yet teems with tiny beings ruined step
by step, mere micro-creatures that our eyes
can't see, so every breath that we inhale
breaks the living chain and kills—and cannot

stop. Jainist monks, equipped with whisk brooms, sweep
their paths and trap their breath in masks they wear
whenever they're outside their cells, afraid
to take a sentient organism's life.
But we are all a part of the great garden,
which waits to make of us a winter pressing.

Eclipse on an August Afternoon, 2017

From the Rose Garden, he watches everyone
rushing from doorways into the open air,
eclipse glasses in hand, in awe of what
they've never seen. Then, as the moon
begins to graze the face of the sun,
the wide sky darkens like evening.

Birds wheeling from tree-tops traverse
the lawn below while strings of lightning bugs
flicker and flit in awkward loops. Still later,
swarming stars infest the upper reaches
and the new moon consumes all but the burning
rim of the sun, an omen like red sky at dawn.

His back to the brink of the Doric portico,
the President gazes up in arrogance
at the visible darkness, bat-blind to
an aide's waving hands, which hold up
the eyewear that enables one to see.

A Silent Scene
In memory of Mike Cavanagh (1942-2017)

Two states away, your service soon
will start. No doubt your printed words,
which have outlasted you—
bronzed men on sculpted horses—
will fill the cloistered hall, but uttered by
another's voice. I can imagine sitting there,
hearing you within the lines, but see
instead a silent scene from years ago:

A foursome walking on the campus green,
a father followed by an elegant brunette
and two tow-headed boys, the April light
brilliant on all their open faces.

The Watchman

*"That the Constables see every House shut up, and to be attended with
Watchmen, which may keep them in . . . for the space of four Weeks
after all be whole."*
                    —Orders by the Lord Mayor, concerning the Plague, 1665

It's a chilly night as dark and still
as London's boneyard when the Deathcart comes
to dump the daily toll. The cart's heaped bodies—
purple and swollen, green with gangrene spots—
shine ghastly in the bellman's glaring torchlight.
The watchman's shift will last till 9 a.m.

Nothing stirs in the muddy street, not even
fleas buried in the fur of rats. All dogs
and cats have been butchered to stop the plague.
All the watchman hears is his own breathing.
Tonight the moon is down, but the red cross
that marks the door still glimmers like a gash.

No one's shown their face since Friday night
when women yelled for him to call the cart,
to carry off a maid they'd wrapped in rugs.
Then Monday afternoon, wailing escaped
an upstairs window; soon an angry man
was screaming for the cart again. Once there,
the carters knocked and knocked, louder each time.

So now it's the night watchman's turn again.
He stands as if in church. He fears what's next,
what's happened in the house, and why it's mute.
At last, before dawn starts to lift the darkness,
he climbs up to the casement, cracks it open,
and calls inside. Hears nothing. Listens harder,
barely making out a metal tinkling,

and sees a simple latch, unhooked and swinging
in the breeze. Suddenly, the silence tolls
like Easter Sunday in the watchman's mind:
Hoisting upward to the ceiling hatch,
the family, leaving their beloved to rot,
had risen, Lazarus-like, from living death,

then crossed a row of rooftops and were gone.

Entrances and Exits

Mother, it's thirty years ago today
you crossed the stage, your second act not over—
and exited. The bare boards, burnished by
your marks, support the players who have followed
not knowing you were there, although you show
us all the way from spotlights into darkness.

With My Late Brother, Mike

It's now been two full years, and spring
        Is back again, as if
You hadn't missed the last two falls—
        A sailor cut adrift.

The robins and the doves arrived
        Just this week, and green
Begins to grow amid the willows,
        A faint but aging sheen.

I have your picture on my desk
        Taken on the yacht
We sailed along the Hudson River
        The year before you got

Too sick to live a normal life.
        Behind you, light blue waters
Glisten and are reflected in
        Your eyes and your granddaughter's.

You're sitting next to your wife, Janice,
        Your arm around her shoulder.
An inner peace lights up your face
        As if you won't grow older.

And yet you could not keep off death.
        So memory, with the weather,
Returns us to the Red Hook harbor
        And our last time together,

Clunking mugs of Michelob
        In a dockside dive—
As if your ship's about to sail
        And you are still alive.

Snow in New York
In memory of my brother Mike

The night I arrived we reminisced till twelve,
and then I slept the deep, long sleep of death—
until the metal scrape on pavement woke
me at three, the room brightened by white,
a quiet, opal otherworldly glow.

Later, in darkness, you rose up to brave
the long commute to get your chemo treatment.
But ice encased the car, like a great glacier
never thawed. You struck and clawed and quarreled
with the cold, stony block, a sculptor scorned
by his hard-hearted muse,
                              then marched us across
the snowy sidewalks to the subway station,
winded in the cutting air but charging
ahead of me whose longest steps kept me
almost behind you.
                    The train ferried us
beneath the buried streets and under the Hudson
to NYU. I watched you doze and held
back tears when Doctor Gu announced, "Six months
and then we need another miracle."
Outside, the buildings scraped the frozen clouds.

You beat the odds, but summer never lasts.
It's winter once again, and snowing in
New York. And though you've since transformed to powder
like night's first falling flakes, you're still ahead
of me, who's following in your footprints.

Intimations: To a Descendant

"The *Talmud* tells us immortality is assured by these things: having a child,
  planting a tree, and writing a book."

—*San Francisco Jung Institute Journal*

When your only child gets sick, so weakened its breathing seems
as shallow as a seed in grass, helplessness will hollow you,
filling the boundless inner space with darkness, broken only
by vaulting hope the sapling will heal.

When middle age arrives, your parents gone, some year the birds
return early, go to the south lawn by the leaning fence,
and a few feet from the stump where the soil mixes with an uncle's ashes,
plant a fast-growing, gritty tulip poplar. Decades from now, in August,
this tree will shade a grateful stranger.

And when winter comes and the hard stars glaze the window
above your chair, you just might light on a wooden shelf
of heirlooms and urns handed down from the nineteenth century.
Here, these last words will rest in a book you'll never read,
like a grave no longer visited.